Yorkshire Past

A special publication brought to you by

YORKSHIRE POST

Additional photographs supplied by

YORKSHIRE Evening Post   Wakefield Express   Harrogate Advertiser   EVENING Courier SCARBOROUGH Evening News

Contents

First published in 2006 by

At Heart Limited
32 Stamford Street,
Altrincham,
Cheshire,
WA14 1EY

in conjunction with
Yorkshire Post Newspapers Ltd
PO Box 168,
Wellington Street,
Leeds,
LS1 1RF

ISBN: 1-84547-106-7

Introduction

Anyone with an acute eye for, and an interest in, history and the way we preserve it, will recognise the essential beauty of *Yorkshire Past*.

Photography is a door through which we can tangibly return to something – a place, a person, a moment in time.

The pictures in this book emphasise the social convulsions of the last hundred years or so, the basic ways in which we now live far differently from our ancestors in regard to dress, employment, transport, entertainment and recreation, and housing.

This bygone age is captured beautifully in the anonymous ploughman, head bent in a baggy grey cap, walking his shire horses down a muddy lane in Healaugh. There's the Hemingbrough smithy, Alfred Teal, peering at us through pebble glasses as he hammers an iron rod against a hulking anvil. There's the knot of entranced Victorian children, impeccably dressed in sailor suits or long white dresses, and smart boaters or sun hats as wide as dustbin lids, who watch a Punch and Judy show at Whitby.

On every page we see life as it used to be.

Look at the tram trundling through turn-of-the-century Halifax, the Queen Mother in her fur wrap at Harewood, and the "boys" in braces drinking tea beside haystacks near York.

The past *is* another country, and things *were* done differently there.

Our fascination with yesteryear has turned nostalgia into a growth pursuit. Whether it is a search for our own family roots, or the task of tracing the changing landscape of a particular town or village, there is an appetite to explore old times.

Yorkshire Past will help you on that journey.

Askham Bryan Planting potatoes near York in 1969 YP001

Askham Richard John Bartram and his son Ray (left) collect straw at the White House Farm in Askham Richard, near York in 1968. The straw was used for bedding cattle during the winter. YP002

Bolton Percy The Old Oak, Appleton Roebuck, May 1950 YP003

Tadcaster This thatched cottage was the home of Miss Prudhoe Peacock of Long Marston. January 1965 YP004

Tadcaster A ploughman makes his way home in Healaugh, near Tadcaster, in February 1931 YP005

York Keith Barley replaces a stained-glass window at Guildhall, after the lead used was corroded by acidic fumes released from the oak pillars used to rebuild the hall in 1960 YP006

York A £8,000 gift from the Italian Embassy to York. Standing 36 feet tall next to the city's art gallery. 1987 YP007

York Monk Bar, 1975 YP008

York The Queen's Hotel, before it was pulled down and rebuilt in replica following a Government decision YP009

York Askham Grange open women's prison, 1968 YP010

York Clifford's Tower pictured in 1955. Its name comes from Roger de Clifford, who was hanged from the top of the tower in 1322. YP011

York Market in Parliament Street before the First World War YP012

York Station in 1934 YP013

York Guildhall, before it was pulled down and rebuilt in 1960 YP014

York Carriage and Wagon Works, 1959 YP015

York Carriage and Wagon Works, 1954 YP016

York A decorated tram in 1910 YP017

York The boys of St Martin's gardening on an allotment, 1925 YP019

York Old farming YP020

Beverley Harry Wright's shop in Westwood Road, which still bears his name. 1950s YP021

Bridlington The Bridlington lifeboat, launching in October 1965 YP022

Bridlington Spa in the early part of the 20th Century YP023

THE HARBOUR, BRIDLINGTON.

Bridlington An early 1900s shot of the pride of Bridlington pleasurecraft fleet, including the Boy's Own, later the Yorkshire Belle, and the Princess Marina steamers YP024

Bridlington A
Coronation Day
parade outside
Bridlington Spa
YP025

Bridlington A
steam locomotive
leaving Bridlington
Station on a
Saturdays-only run
to Rotherham
Central, August
1955 YP026

Bridlington Nurses parade past the spa on Coronation Day YP027

Bridlington A cheeky postcard from the 1920s to prove holidays in Bridlington were definitely the latest thing YP028

Driffield Haymakers on the lawn at Sledmere House in 1888 YP029

Filey The Rev. E. Eglen, left, a Methodist minister, and the Rev. Wilfred Curtis, Church of England, jointly conduct a service of dedication for the new Filey lifeboat watched by members of the crew, towns people and visitors to the resort in 1968 YP030

Hemingbrough Lund, January 1973 YP031

Hemingbrough Mr Alfred Teal at The Old Red Brick Smithy YP032

Hemingbrough Lunds church, Nidderdale, near the source of the Ure, March 1968 YP033

Holme-on-Spalding-Moor Mr George Morton's 138 acre farm in 1971. This was one of the last farms to use shire horses. YP034

Hull The success of Priestman's first small dredging crane bought by Hull Dock Company in 1878 led to orders from all over the world. A century on, an exhibition, 'Priestman's Hundred Years of Success', was opened. YP035

Hull Bull Sand Fort in the River Humber, 1964 YP036

Hull A postcard showing trawlers that had been fired upon during the 'Russian Outrage' in the North Sea in 1904, back in port in St Andrew's dock YP037

Hull The World War II bomb being removed from the factory site at Shipham and Company, Hawthorn Avenue, five years after it had been dropped in 1942 YP038

Hull Docks, 1930 YP039

Hull Corporation Pier in 1928 YP040

Hull Queen's Dock which was filled in during the early 1920s YP041

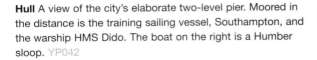

Hull A view of the city's elaborate two-level pier. Moored in the distance is the training sailing vessel, Southampton, and the warship HMS Dido. The boat on the right is a Humber sloop. YP042

Hull The first cars to cross the Humber Bridge, 1981 YP043

Hull The Queen and Duke of Edinburgh at the opening of the Humber Bridge in 1981 YP044

Hull Humber Bridge in construction, February 1978 YP045

Hull The Humber Bridge, March 1980 YP046

Hull Queen's Gardens 1965 YP047

Hull The main entrance to Hull Fair in Walton Street, October 1948 YP048

Hull Joe Buchan, son of the Humber lifeboat captain, closes the gate leading to Spurn Point in December 1967, due to the foot and mouth epidemic YP049

Hull A 1950s photograph of Carnival Day at the Sailors' Families' Society's Newland Estate, which was put up for sale in 2004 YP050

Hull The Earl de Grey public house, right of the picture, in Castle Street in the 1950s YP051

Hull Entrance to the prison, October 1966 YP052

Hull Local man, Mr John G. Theilman, whose parents lived in Westbourne Avenue, North Ferriby, piloted Britain's first helicopter mail service, an experiment to make deliveries to isolated parts of Yorkshire and the North of England. June 1948 YP053

Kilnsea The lighthouse at Spurn Head
YP054

Kilnsea Spurn Head, home of the
lifeboat workers YP055

Kilnsea The lifeboatmen's cottages at
Spurn Point, May 1964 YP056

Kilnsea The new coastguard station at Spurn Point, November 1976 YP057

Kirby Underdale Garrowby Hill, always a menace to motorists in winter, nestling under the first snow of 1967 YP058

Kirby Underdale Snow on Fridaythorpe Road, 1968 YP059

Rudston Farming at Rudston, five miles from Bridlington, circa 1910 YP060

South Cave Little Wold Plantation, a distinctive landmark rich in birdlife and flowers, February 1994 YP061

South Cave Town Hall in May 1971 YP062

Arkengarthdale Arkle looking westwards, June 1959 YP063

Bedale Planting potatoes at Snape Lodge Farm, 1962 YP064

Fylingthorpe village, 1966 YP065

Fylingdales View from the top of the Devil's Elbow, looking towards the Moor where an American ballistic missile early warning base was eventually built. In the centre is the Saltersgate farmhouse. February 1960 YP066

Fylingdales Construction of the early warning base, October 1962 YP067

Fylingdales The completed warning system YP068

Gilling East Post box, Cawton, October 1971 YP069

Grinton A view from the edge of the moors above Grinton, looking north across
Swaledale. In the centre is Reeth. October 1963 YP070

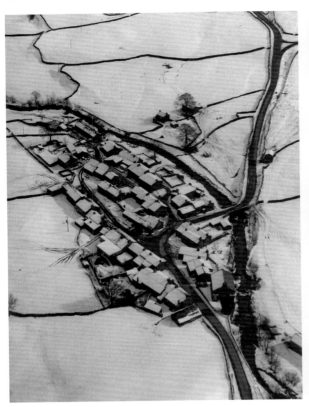

Grinton Keld in Swaledale, 1969
YP071

Guisborough Priory, July 1963 YP072

Guisborough A view looking towards
the Priory, July 1963 YP073

Hinderwell Women watching the boats come in, taken at
Staithes in July 1888 YP074

Hinderwell Staithes on the North Yorkshire Coast, 1967
YP075

Hinderwell A fisherwoman sewing in Runswick YP076

Malton Evening Post reporter Keith Nicholson looks at his
watch as he crosses the road at Butcher Corner, December
1967 YP077

Middleham The village centre, July 1951 YP078

Middleham The Ure Bridge, September 1967 YP079

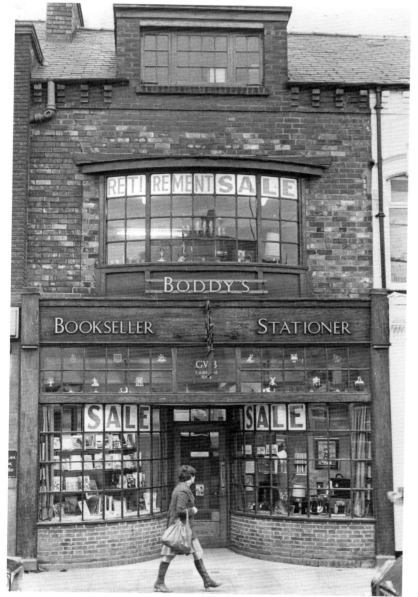

Middleham Castle in the 1950s YP080

Middleham The Castle with the Queen Victoria jubilee fountain in the foreground, June 1969 YP081

Middlesbrough Boddy's book and stationery shop, December 1975 YP082

Middleton High Force in the 1960s YP083

Middleton View looking down from Dent Bank with the
River Tees running fairly high after the recent rains. March
1964 YP084

Scarborough in the 1950s YP085

Scarborough in the 1970s YP086

Scarborough Aquarium top, 1950s YP087

Scarborough The town in the early 20th Century YP088

Scarborough in the 19th Century
YP089

Scarborough Harbour YP090

Scarborough Foreshore Road in the
19th Century YP091

Scarborough A busy North Bay in 1967
YP092

Scarborough The Spa in 1968 YP093

Scarborough Some of the herring boats in harbour, 1967
YP094

Scarborough Southbay Beach YP095

Scarborough Royal Albert Drive
YP096

Scarborough The herring fleet at the
harbour, 1968 YP097

Scarborough Peasholm Park in the 1950s YP098

Scarborough Royal Albert Drive YP099

Thirsk Part of the village green at Sowerby, where the effects of a Mr Cornish were auctioned outside his home at 89 Front Street in June 1971 YP100

Thirsk St Peter's Church, Sowerby, pictured in 1960 YP101

Thorton Dale Low Dalby, near Thorton Dale, July 1970 YP102

Thorton Dale One of the views of the forest drive, hauling pit props from the woodland at Low Dalby, March 1964 YP103

West Tanfield Threshing and baling at mill farm, near Masham, 1955 YP104

Whitby Busy beach scene around the turn of the 20th Century YP105

Whitby A traditional seaside Punch and Judy show in 1875 YP106

Whitby Mulgrave Castle Inn between Whitby and Sandsend, pictured in the late 19th Century, was a regular smugglers' haunt YP107

Whitby Fishergirls examining newly landed herring YP108

Whitby Looking down Lythe Bank from Lythe, October 1961 YP109

Aberford Threshing time at a local farm in November 1936 YP110

Aldborough Potato scratters at Hundayfield Farm, Boroughbridge YP111

Aldborough Smith's farm, Branton Green, 1917 YP112

Almondbury The new methodist church, February 1969 YP113

Armthorpe The local church with Markham Main Colliery in the background, March 1968 YP114

Barwick In Elmet Old Cottages on Austhorpe Road, Cross Gates, in 1895 YP115

Batley Garry Walker (right) and his friends Glen and Justin, all aged four, sit on a wall and watch barley being harvested at Stillhouse Farm in Upper Batley. 1969 YP116

Bentham Sixth former Paul Bradbury of Bentham Grammar School on crossing patrol duty watched by Police Constable George Marshall (right), who is also giving advice to sixth formers. May 1969 YP117

Birstall Major Gwen Wyatt and Lt. Audrey Bartlett of the Birstall Salvation Army in December 1987. The pair became widely known as "the mobile army", for they were a familiar sight travelling around the district on a motor scooter. YP118

Birstall Lumb Hall near Drighlington, September 1964
YP119

Bradford An aerial view of 1959 YP120

Bradford Aerial view of Shipley, May 1959 YP121

Bradford Views of Bradford from
February 1969 YP122

Bradford Panoramic view of Shipley
shopping centre, October 1960 YP123

Bradford Locals of Shipley Glen, circa
1900 YP124

Bradford Floods in Cheapside, July 1968 YP125

Bradford Apperley Bridge, Ferncliffe, better known to TV viewers as Champion House, which was put up for sale in 1968 YP126

Bradford The quiet winter scene on the Leeds Liverpool Canal at Apperley Bridge, near Bradford. In the background is the Apperley Road swing bridge. 1968 YP127

Bradford Appleby Bridge, August 1970 YP128

Bradford Mr Hugh Wallace of Greengates and his children David (aged two) and Christine (aged four) and their friend, nine year old Joyce Copper, pause to admire the cabin cruisers moored along the canal bank at Apperley Bridge. April 1961 YP129

Bradford Huge stocks of large size coal stacked high along the roadside at Allerton Bywater, December 1958 YP130

Bradford The pavilion of Bradford Park Avenue Cricket Ground. 1966 YP131

Bradford Almost deserted stands at Bradford Park Avenue Football Ground for the team's Division 4 game against Newport County YP132

Bradford The town's first black bus conductress, Miss Christine Humphreys, in the 1960s YP133

Bradford Two police cars with the new blue flashing beacons which replaced the more familiar police signs. April 1963 YP134

Bramham Boston Spa Primary School Crossing, October 1968 YP135

Brotherton Removal of 215 yards of the Brotherton tunnel between Burton Salmon and Ferrybridge Stations in 1952 YP136

Burnsall The controversial house of Mrs Jean Williams at Appletreewick in the
Yorkshire Dales. December 1969 YP137

Burnsall This beautiful reredos at Appletreewick in Wharfedale was the work of
the Burnsall Village craftsmen. It was made of oak beams from Old Gladstone
Hall. April 1933 YP138

Burnsall Looking towards Appletreewick from the Bolton Abbey to Burnsall Road.
On the right is Simon's Seat. November 1959 YP139

Burnsall The Old Mill at Hartlington, May 1965 YP140

Burnsall A village scene in Appletreewick in Wharfedale, May 1973 YP141

Burnsall A 17th Century granary at Low Hall, Appletreewick, houses a remarkable collection of relics of Nidderdale's farming past. March 1971 YP142

Calverley This wintry scene was pictured at
Woodhall Hills, on the Calverley to Pudsey
road in February 1968 YP143

Carleton in Craven Lothersdale, near Skipton,
February 1978 YP144

Carleton in Craven The hills of Lothersdale in
1972 YP145

Carleton in Craven The grassy slopes of
Lothersdale, July 1960 YP146

Castleford A "train" of containers, laden with coal from Allerton Bywater Colliery is being towed by tug on the canal near Castleford, and is passing an empty "train" which is returning to pick up another load. 1955 YP147

Castleford Glasshoughton Colliery, April 1964 YP148

Cawthorne Harvesting at the Barhow's
in the early 20th Century YP149

Dewsbury The town centre, October
1962 YP150

Dewsbury The Old Bus Station YP151

Dewsbury The New Central Fire
Station in 1964 YP152

Dewsbury Three long-serving
employees, all locals, who worked as
cutters in the reception sidings at
Dewsbury Marshalling Yards. From left
to right: Clifford Collier (48 years'
service), Sid Newsome (42 years'
service) and Fred Horne (40 years'
service). 1964 YP153

Dewsbury Railway Yard on Wellington
Road YP154

Dewsbury M1 intersection construction at Flushdyke, Ossett, 1967 YP155

Dewsbury The Sheffield to Leeds M1 motorway between Horbury and Ossett in 1965 YP156

Dewsbury The M1 from Leeds enters the picture from the bottom, and the first intersection is with the A638 Dewsbury (off right) to Wakefield Road, where a link roundabout with the M1 was being constructed. The next intersection is with Queens Drive, Ossett. YP157

Dewsbury Flooded roads outside the Playhouse Cinema YP158

Doncaster Installing anchor piles on the Sheffield and South Yorkshire Navigation improvement scheme at Spotborough in April 1980 YP159

Doncaster A pedestrian crossing in July 1961, before the by-pass was built YP160

Featherstone Whitwood Colliery, 1968 YP161

Ferry Fryston A hayfield in Airedale, between Keighley and Skipton in 1926 YP162

Garforth Mrs Tilly Bullough helps children to safely cross the road at the junction of Main Street and Church Lane, July 1965 YP163

Giggleswick Stainforth Force, near Settle, March 1971 YP164

Guiseley The first day of Yeadon Market in Town Hall Square. August 1971 YP165

Guiseley Members of Leeds City Police ride motorcycles for the first time on a private road at the Carlton Motoring Instruction Centre in Yeadon, under the supervision of Sgt. Anthony Bebb (right) and PC Raymond Dobson (left). June 1966 YP166

Guiseley Mrs Lock (left) with fellow members of the Civic Society, Mr Dick Gibbon and Mrs Anne Barnes, admire the "long stoop", a Roman landmark that was relocated from its original 500 year-old home to make way for the runway extension. 1984 YP167

Guiseley Yeadon Stoop at its original location, the junction of Warren House Lane and Harrogate Road in 1957 YP168

Guiseley The restaurant at Harry Ramsden's in 1964 YP169

Guiseley An external view of the new extension at Harry Ramsden's in 1968 YP170

Halifax A view of the town taken from nearby Pule Hill in 1966 YP171

Halifax Piece Hall, 1964 YP172

Halifax Elland Bridge, circa 1910 YP173

Halifax Dean Clough, Crossleys YP174

Halifax A tram trundles through the town's streets around the turn of the century YP175

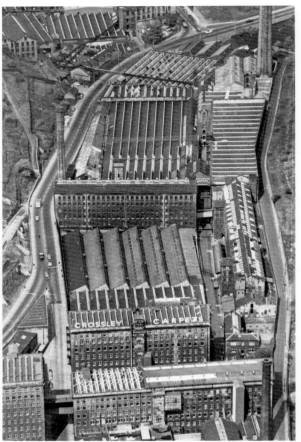

Halifax Behind Elland Town Hall, 1911 YP176

Halifax The opening of the town hall in
Hipperholme in 1899 YP177

Halifax Hipperholme Methodist Church in the
1900s YP178

Halifax George Corner, 1904 YP179

Halifax Old King Cross Street in the early 1900s YP180

Halifax The Grand Theatre in the 1890s YP181

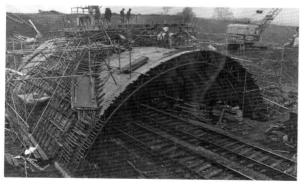

Halifax Park Street, 1929 YP182

Halifax Work in progress on the bridge over the Leeds-Bradford line at New Pudsey Station. 1967 YP183

Halifax Lancestan Street, 1963 YP184

Halifax Victoria Hall, 1960 YP185

Halifax The demolition of the Palace Theatre in 1959 YP186

Halifax The town centre in 1961 YP187

Halifax Southowram Bank, September 1961 YP188

Halifax Part of the city is cleared in 1966 YP189

Halifax Thornton Square at Brighouse, looking towards the Anchor Bridge, along
Briggate towards Rastrick. February 1965 YP190

Halifax Gibbet Street Post Office in the 1960s YP191

Halifax Police on the look out for clues in Barkisland to help solve the murder of Margaret Victoria Williamson in 1964 YP192

Halifax Hebden Bridge viewed from the Birchcliffe hillside looking towards Todmorden, November 1976 YP193

Halifax Gibson Mill, Hardcastle Craggs, September 1976 YP194

Halifax The town centre viewed from Southowram Bank in 1972 YP195

Halifax Low Lane, Lower Skircoat, April 1974 YP196

Halifax The new police headquarters at Sowerby Bridge from where Detective Chief Superintendent Lodge and his team conducted their enquiries after vacating premises at the Mill at Barkisland. December 1964 YP197

Halifax The Mayor of Calderdale hands over to Mr C. A. Ramsden the mallet with which the foundation stone was laid at the town hall's centenary celebrations in 1963 YP198

Halifax A lone lorry on the bleak Halifax to Rochdale road near Baitings Reservoir in 1960. Snow drifts blocked many roads in Yorkshire that winter, and many more were made hazardous by ice and driving winds. YP199

Halifax A 'road closed' notice at Ripponden, near Halifax, in 1969. The closure applied to both the Oldham and Rochdale routes over the Pennines. YP200

Halifax Luddenden Vale, looking up the valley from above Booth. June 1948 YP201

Halifax Apple House, Stocks Lane, Luddenden in 1967 YP202

Halifax Heptonstall, April 1964 YP203

Halifax The headquarters of Sagar-Richards Limited nestled in the Calder Valley below the busy Halifax-Burnley road at Luddenden Foot. June 1969 YP204

Harewood The Queen Mother plants a tree while visiting Harewood House in the 1950s YP205

Hemsworth Kinsley evictions YP206

Holme Moss A snowy scene in 1968 on the A6024 near the Yorkshire-Cheshire boundary, close to the BBC transmitter, looking towards Holmfirth and Huddersfield YP207

Huddersfield A view of the Queen Victoria Memorial Tower in November 1966 YP208

Huddersfield Queen Street Mission, January 1971 YP209

Huddersfield The New College of Technology, November 1960 YP210

Huddersfield The town's second police headquarters – combined with the old fire station – in Peel Street in September 1968, which was soon to be demolished to make way for the New Market Hall YP211

Huddersfield town centre, August 1973 YP212

Huddersfield The River Colne at Clough Lee Mills, Marsden, June 1969 YP213

Huddersfield The old and the new, with the ultra modern Market Hall
development in the foreground, August 1974 YP214

Huddersfield Law Courts and Police Headquarters, August 1973 YP215

Huddersfield The new fire station, Upperhead Row, February 1961 YP216

Huddersfield The exterior of the assembly shop at Cliffe & Co. Ltd Engineers, Longroyd Bridge, December 1970 YP217

Huddersfield The finishing touches are applied to the exterior of the new Midland Bank premises, June 1970 YP218

Huddersfield Tulips in bloom at Greenhead Park, May 1955 YP219

Huddersfield Greenhead Park, February 1946 YP220

Huddersfield Lion statue guards the town, February 1969 YP221

Huddersfield An aerial view of the town centre, August 1953 YP222

Huddersfield The town's first police station, at the corner of Victoria Street and Bull and Mouth Street, September 1968 YP223

Huddersfield Sculptured frontage to the new Market Hall in August 1970 YP224

Huddersfield The Theatre Royal, March 1961 YP225

Huddersfield Looking towards Shambles Lane, June 1953 YP226

Huddersfield Croslands Mill and
industrial works, January 1946 YP227

Huddersfield Market Place in April 1947
YP228

Huddersfield New buildings off
Manchester Road YP229

Huddersfield Work being carried out on the Scammonden Dam on the M62 in May 1968 YP230

Huddersfield Section of the 129 ft high Lockwood Viaduct in 1938 YP231

Huddersfield Two men narrowly escaped death when this railway coach broke loose from a siding near Lockwood Station in June 1958. The coach ran down a gradient, crashing through buffers and the bridge parapet into the road below, before finishing up in the station booking hall across the road. YP232

Huddersfield The head of a mile long queue of vehicles held up by snow at Marsden, just below Standedge, in February 1958 YP233

Huddersfield Standedge blizzards, 1966 YP234

Huddersfield The view looking West at Milnsbridge, November 1968 YP235

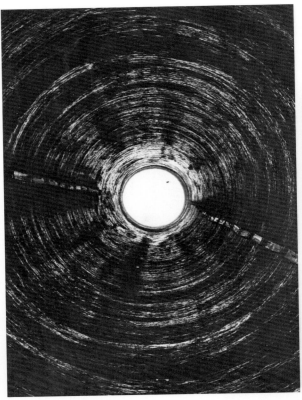

Huddersfield The 450ft deep Brun Clough airshaft at Standedge railway tunnel on the border of Yorkshire and Lancashire in 1966 YP236

Huddersfield Railwaymen John Moore and George Hopper wait in a recess in the depths of the Standedge Tunnel as a steam train clatters past. 1966 YP237

Ilkley This picture of Brook Street was taken the day after the iron railway bridge was removed YP238

Ilkley Hundreds of locals enjoy the facilities of the town's outdoor swimming pool YP239

Ilkley Miss Gay Wright, aged 18, of Brook Street, Ilkley, posts Christmas mail in an unusual six-sided pillar-box sited in Denton Road, Ilkley. Designed by Mr J. W. Penfold, the box was originally erected in Bradford in 1875. December 1971 YP240

Ilkley Cow and claf rocks YP241

Kirkby Malhamdale Cyclists resting at Malham in the late 1950s YP242

Kirkby Overblow Stainburn Church looking over Wharfedale, January 1968 YP243

Kirkby Overblow Stainburn Church of England Primary School, June 1965 YP244

Knaresborough Known locally as Hell Hole Rock, this rock is one of many outcrops in the district, and is supposed to have played a part in the initiation of Druid children into Rock Worship. October 1949 YP245

Ledsham Lawn and gardens at the Ledston Luck Colliery near Kippax, June 1955 YP246

Leeds West Bar, Boar Lane in the early 20th Century YP247

Leeds Boar Lane in the early 1900s YP248

Leeds Norton's Oyster Shop on Boar Lane at the turn of the century YP249

Leeds A view of Boar Lane taken from Briggate, March 1928 YP250

Leeds Saxone shoe shop stands at the corner of Briggate around 1900 YP251

Leeds The Corn Exchange on Briggate in the 19th Century YP252

Leeds Briggate in the late 19th Century YP253

Leeds McConnell's wine bar in Briggate, March 1959 YP254

Leeds The Odeon cinema on the corner of New Briggate and The Headrow in 1951 YP255

Leeds Leeds Arcades at the Victoria Quarter at the junction between Briggate and Boar Lane YP256

Leeds The old Upper Headrow in the late 1920s YP257

Leeds The site of The Merrion Centre, showing the great fire-fighting water tank in 1945 YP258

Leeds Prisoners on the roof at Armley Jail in 1911 YP259

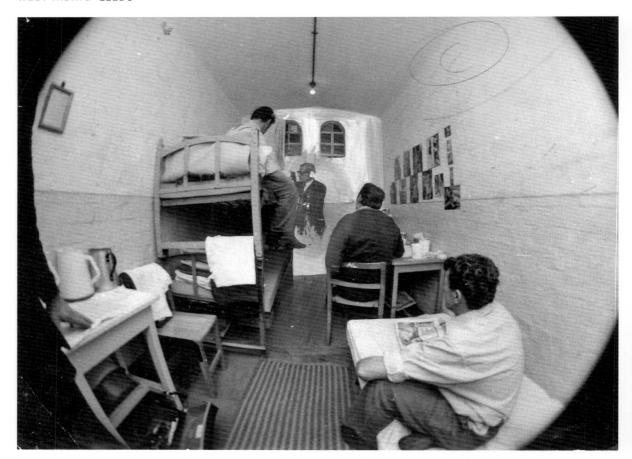

Leeds A cell at Armley Jail on New Year's Eve 1970 YP260

Leeds Fred Walker and the flogging stool, last used in 1926, at Armley Jail, August 1972 YP261

Leeds The Christmas mail rush at Leeds General Post Office, November 1935 YP262

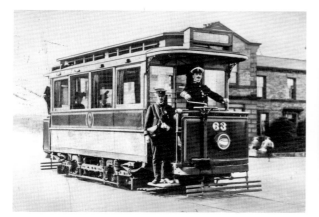

Leeds A single-deck tramcar in 1905
YP263

Leeds Trams make their way past
Timpson's show shop towards West
Park YP264

Leeds Bus driver Malcolm Brian
demonstrates the two-way radio
system in 1964 YP265

Leeds Cheerful driver Brian Walker on Leeds City Transport's 79 bus route between Pudsey and Horsforth in 1971 YP266

Leeds Coach conductress, Mrs Clara Hodgson, prepares for her retirement in 1972 after almost 25 years' service with the West Yorkshire Road Car Company YP267

Leeds A B1 Class North Allerton steam train at Central Railway Station, March 1957 YP268

Leeds A Headrow policeman on the beat is given details of an occurrence by a motorcycle patrol officer, September 1965 YP269

Leeds Cleaning out the train compartments at the Neville Hill Rail Depot in 1953 YP270

Leeds The new and improved Leeds Bradford Airport, following building work in the 1960s YP271

Leeds A view from the top of the new control tower at Leeds Bradford Airport in 1966 YP272

Leeds On the tarmac at Leeds Bradford Airport in the 1960s YP273

Leeds Oxy-acetylene flares had to be used to assist the police on traffic control duty during heavy fog in 1958 YP274

Leeds Snow holds up traffic on the Leeds to Dewsbury road in March 1969 YP275

Leeds Clarence Dock around 1950 YP276

Leeds The Great Yorkshire Show at Temple Newsam, just outside Leeds, in July 1932. One of the attractions there, for the first time, was a collection of sixty pit ponies from the West Riding and South Yorkshire coal mines. YP277

Leeds Harrogate Road in Chapel
Allerton in the early 1900s YP278

Leeds Harvest in Scott Hall Road,
Moor Allerton, August 1932 YP279

Leeds Farming work on the
outskirts of the city in 1966 YP280

Long Preston This wrought iron trophy was presented to the village for winning the best kept village competition, organised by the Yorkshire Rural Community Council, in 1972 YP281

Long Preston Traffic on the Settle Road passes through the village, August 1969 YP282

Long Preston This horse chestnut tree was the centre of a dispute between the local council and local man Fred Reylands, who had trimmed some of the branches of the tree to make way for an extension to the premises of his antiques shop in Main Street in July 1974 YP283

Low Bentham The historic Ribblehead
viaduct YP284

Low Bentham The Ribblehead
viaduct, photographed in 1956 YP285

Methley Savile Colliery in 1963 YP286

Morley Fire at Albion Mills in 1961 YP287

Morley The mill fire that led to the town hall catching light in 1961 YP288

Normanton Altofts Colliery in 1963 prior to its demolition YP289

Normanton Europe's longest unbroken row of
three-storey terraced houses on Silkstone Row,
Altofts, 1975 YP290

Normanton The back yards of the mill houses on
Silkstone Row in 1975 YP291

Otley A view of the town from January 1967 YP292

Otley A view from Otley Chevin, May 1960 YP293

Otley This idyllic scene was captured near the bridge over the Wharfe in August 1968 YP294

Otley Industry and rural life live in harmony in this view of the weir on the River Wharfe from June 1968 YP295

Pontefract The streets and terraced houses of Tanshelf were rapidly disappearing when this photograph was taken in 1967 YP296

Ripon John Taylor does some ploughing at Melrose Farm, Bishop Monkton, near Ripon in 1960 YP297

Ripon A lead mine in the Yorkshire Dales, Greenhow Hill YP298

Ripon A 1950s view of the town hall
and marketplace YP299

Rotherham Pouring has just finished at
Steel, Peech & Tozer melting shop,
Templeborough, 1954 YP300

Rotherham Police and pickets at the
Templeborough Rolling Mills, during the
1980s steel strike YP301

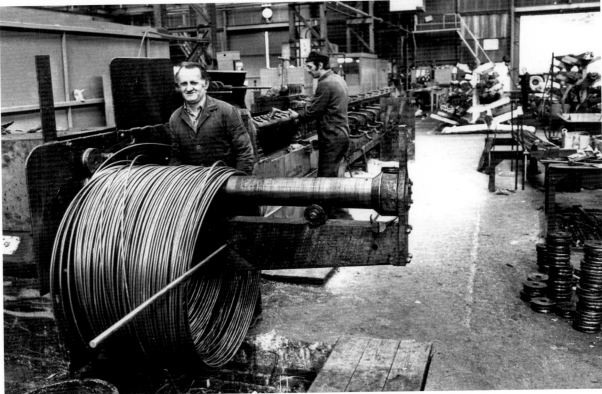

Rothwell Work is carried out on the M62 at Oulton in 1969
YP302

Selby The Ship Inn on the banks of the River Ouse in Long
Drax near Selby, August 1959 YP303

Sheffield Kiveton Park Steel works, April 1981 YP304

Sheffield Pickets at Moore and Wrights, during the steel strike of 1980 YP305

Sheffield Picket line in Sheffied during the steel strikes, Feb 1980 YP306

Sheffield Grinding high speed twist drills at Arthur Balfour Steel Works, Broughton Lane, Attercliffe, March 1946 YP307

Sheffield Arthur Balfour Steel Works, Broughton Lane, Attercliffe, December 1954 YP308

Sheffield Forging high carbon steel at Arthur Balfour Steel Works in March 1946 YP309

Sheffield The cutlery workshop at Samuel Peace & Sons Limited YP310

Sheffield The unveiling of the 1966 blade for the Joseph Rodgers knife is performed by Mrs Sylvia Kaiser, July 1966 YP311

Sheffield The World Cup comes to the city as West Germany play Switzerland at Hillsborough in July 1966 YP312

Sheffield West Germany's Franz Beckenbauer runs the ball past Uruguay keeper, Mazurkieviez, during the World Cup Quarter Final match on 23 July 1966 YP313

Sheffield Match referee Jim Finney stands hands on hips as Uruguay captain, Troche, leaves the field after being sent off at Hillsborough, July 1966 YP314

Sheffield The 1966 World Cup Liason Committee meet at Sheffield YP315

Sherburn in Elmet Grinding fodder for the farm stock at Huddleston Hall, 1902 YP316

Sherburn in Elmet Steeton Hall Gateway, South Milford, October 1959 YP317

Sherburn in Elmet Subsidence in West View in Micklefield, February 1978 YP318

Sherburn in Elmet Peckfield Colliery, Micklefield, May 1975 YP319

Silkstone A television camera (ringed) watches the operation of a coal conveying belt 240 feet down Dodworth Colliery. The picture is received in the control room. February 1966 YP320

Skipton Manby's premises in High Street, which the firm first occupied in 1817. August 1967 YP321

Skipton Alison Christie, three, and her sister Julie, four, of Walton Street, on a shopping trip to Ilkley, use the 100 year old postbox in Denton Road, to post their Christmas mail. The box designed by Mr J. W. Penfold is hexagonal in shape. December 1971 YP322

Skipton Springs canal, 1958 YP323

Skipton After seven years of "retirement" from Skipton Castle, Mr Wilfred Ash, 81, was still going strong in August 1960. Here he tells the story of the historic building he has known so intimately for 51 years to a new generation. YP324

Skipton Cottages in Back Water Street, 1968 YP325

Skipton One of the town centre's new traffic signs, 1969 YP326

South Kirkby Colliery in 1966 YP327

South Kirkby A roadside view from November 1966 YP328

South Stainley The work of removing the remains of the old railway bridge was interrupted because of a gas dispute. February 1973 YP329

South Stainley Stainley House in April 1973 YP330

Spofforth Follifoot Village in 1962 YP331

Spofforth The main street in August 1951 YP332

Spofforth Spofforth Church in need of restoration in March
1957 YP333

Spofforth Spofforth Hall under reconstruction into a
Cheshire Home for incurables in February 1959 YP334

Thorne Colliery near Doncaster.
1967 YP335

Thorne 5,000 acres of farm and
marsh land being protected for the
development of a regional airport.
October 1968 YP336

Thorne, Market Place and King
Street, June 1972 YP337

Thorne King Street, June 1972 YP338

Thorner Main village street, October 1968 YP339

Thorner The Parish Church in December 1965 YP340

Thorner Stream which runs by the
footpath in Westfield Lane. September
1961 YP341

Wakefield The new pithead at
Newmillerdam Colliery, November 1960
YP342

Wakefield Street scenes from the top of
Westgate, January 1977 YP343

Wakefield A British Rail high speed train in the 1970s YP344

Wakefield Six mini-vans ready to go into operation with Wakefield City Police. May 1968 YP345

Wakefield Tammy Hall Street, June 1975 YP346

Wakefield Little Westgate in June 1975
YP347

Wakefield Full-back Cooper is tackled by Bradford Northern forward Fisher (no. 9) during a game at Belle Vue, October 1969 YP348

Wakefield Trinity final team at Wembley in 1946. Back row: Exley, Teall, Croston, Higgins, Howes, Larson, Bratley, Wilkinson. Bottom row: Baddeley, Goodfellow, Stott, Jones, Rylance. YP349

Wakefield The Victorian gatehouse at Wakefield Prison in August 1973 YP350

Wakefield The long bare galleries of a prison wing, each floor separated by safety netting, under the eye of a watchful prison officer. June 1960 YP351

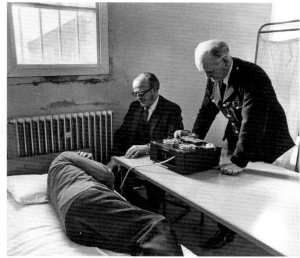

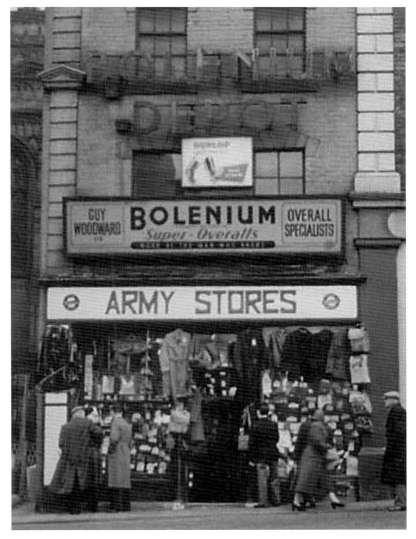

Wakefield Members of the Wakefield jail football team training on their £10,000 all-weather pitch in February 1972 YP352

Wakefield Dr Peter Smith Moorhouse supervises a hypnotherapy session for alcoholics at Wakefield Prison helped by Mr Joseph Kaveney, the prison hospital principal officer (right). November 1971 YP353

Wakefield Army Stores, 1957 YP354

Wakefield The West Riding Operatic Society's Show Boat hits the stage in 1964 YP355

Wakefield The Square in 1965 YP356

Woodkirk A long span of bridge which would eventually form part of the Yorkshire-Lancashire motorway, stands at the side of the Wakefield-Bradford road near Tingley crossroads. July 1968 YP357